foreword

Long before early settlers brightened holiday tables with a dish of jewel-toned cranberry sauce, North American aboriginals used this tart, indigenous fruit for everything from medicine and dyes to a long-lasting food source. Today, savvy cooks know that these bright red berries deserve more than just side-dish status at a turkey dinner, and find ways to use them in a variety of savoury and sweet dishes.

At Company's Coming, we've compiled some of our favourite recipes from our files to create this convenient book. Whether it's an appetizer or a salad, an easy chicken entree or fruit-studded cornbread, you'll find delicious ideas on the following pages. We've even included a fabulous Cran-Orange Chutney recipe to pair with the festive turkey, so you can satisfy all your cranberry cravings!

Jean Paré

cranberry cheese

You can use a mold or even a large cookie cutter to shape this spread. Serve with crackers or Melba toast.

Grated sharp white Cheddar cheese, softened	2 cups	500 mL
Cream cheese, softened	4 oz.	125 g
Dried cranberries, coarsely chopped	1/4 cup	60 mL

Beat Cheddar cheese and cream cheese in medium bowl until smooth.

Add cranberries. Stir. Press into ungreased 1 1/2 cup (375 mL) mold, packing well to avoid air spaces. Cover with plastic wrap. Chill for at least 3 hours until firm. Loosen from mold and invert onto small serving plate. Serves 10.

1 serving: 137 Calories; 11.2 g Total Fat (1.1 g Mono, 0.1 g Poly, 6.5 g Sat); 36 mg Cholesterol; 4 g Carbohydrate; trace Fibre; 6 g Protein; 178 mg Sodium

holiday whirls

These appetizers have the festive colours of red, white and green. Serve on a bed of mint leaves.

Crumbled feta cheese, room temperature	1 3/4 cups	425 mL
Block of cream cheese, softened	8 oz.	250 g
Chopped dried cranberries	1 cup	250 mL
Finely chopped fresh mint (or green onion)	1/4 cup	60 mL
Spinach flour tortillas (10 inch, 25 cm, diameter)	5	5

Cream feta cheese and cream cheese in medium bowl.

Add cranberries and mint. Stir.

Spread about 1/2 cup (125 mL) cheese mixture on each tortilla to within 1/2 inch (12 mm) of edge. Roll up tightly, jelly roll-style. Cover each roll with plastic wrap. Chill for at least 6 hours or overnight. Trim ends. Cut each roll diagonally into 8 slices. Makes 40 slices.

1 slice: 65 Calories; 4 g Total Fat (1.0 g Mono, 0.3 g Poly, 2.2 g Sat); 11.5 mg Cholesterol; 5 g Carbohydrate; 1 g Fibre; 2 g Protein; 121 mg Sodium

cranberry meatballs

Make sure to have toothpicks and napkins on hand if you're serving these as finger food. Also well-received at any potluck dinner.

Large eggs, fork-beaten	2	2
Cornflake crumbs	1 cup	250 mL
Finely chopped onion	1/2 cup	125 mL
Soy sauce	2 tbsp.	30 mL
Parsley flakes	1 tbsp.	15 mL
Garlic cloves, minced (or 1/2 tsp., 2 mL, powder)	2	2
Salt	2 tsp.	10 mL
Pepper	1/2 tsp.	2 mL
Lean ground beef	2 lbs.	900 g
Can of whole cranberry sauce	14 oz.	398 mL
Chili sauce	1/2 cup	125 mL
Ketchup	1/2 cup	125 mL
Brown sugar, packed	2 tbsp.	30 mL
White vinegar	1 tbsp.	15 mL

Combine first 8 ingredients in large bowl.

Add beef. Mix well. Roll into 1 inch (2.5 cm) balls. Place in greased 3 quart (3 L) casserole.

Combine remaining 5 ingredients in small bowl. Pour over meatballs. Bake, uncovered, in 350°F (175°C) oven for about 45 minutes until meatballs are fully cooked and internal temperature reaches 160°F (71°C). Makes about 80 meatballs.

4 meatballs: 182 Calories; 7.4 g Total Fat (3.2 g Mono, 0.4 g Poly, 2.9 g Sat); 47 mg Cholesterol; 19 g Carbohydrate; 1 g Fibre; 10 g Protein; 650 mg Sodium

mulled cranberry juice

This recipe is easily doubled or tripled when carollers or company come to your door.

Cranberry cocktail	4 cups	1 L
Granulated sugar	1/4 cup	60 mL
Lemon juice	2 tbsp.	30 mL
Whole allspice	10	10
Cinnamon stick (4 inches, 10 cm)	1	1

Combine all 5 ingredients in medium saucepan. Bring to a boil. Reduce heat to medium. Boil gently, uncovered, for 5 minutes, stirring occasionally. Strain through sieve into heavy glasses. Makes about 4 cups (1 L).

1 cup (250 mL): 193 Calories; 0.3 g Total Fat (trace Mono, 0.1 g Poly, trace Sat); 0 mg Cholesterol; 49 g Carbohydrate; trace Fibre; trace Protein; 5 mg Sodium

cranberry lemon sipper

Start this lovely aperitif in November, so you'll have a ready supply to sip over the holidays or tuck into someone's stocking. Serve as is, or mixed with ginger ale, club soda or sparkling water for a festive spritzer.

Fresh (or frozen, thawed) cranberries	4 cups	1 L
Granulated sugar	2 cups	500 mL
Water	1 cup	250 mL
Sweet white wine (such as Gewürztraminer)	2 cups	500 mL
Vodka	1 1/2 cups	375 mL
Grated zest and juice of 1 medium lemon (see Tip, page 64)		

Combine first 3 ingredients in large saucepan. Bring to a boil, stirring often. Reduce heat to medium. Boil gently, uncovered, for 5 to 10 minutes, stirring occasionally, until cranberries are softened. Remove from heat.

Add remaining 3 ingredients. Stir well. Cool. Pour into sterile 10 cup (2.5 L) jar with tight-fitting lid. Let stand at room temperature for 3 weeks, shaking gently once every 2 days. Strain through sieve into large bowl. Do not press. Gently lift cranberry mixture with spoon, allowing liquid to flow through sieve. Discard solids. Strain liquid again through double layer of cheesecloth into 8 cup (2 L) liquid measure. Pour into sterile jars or decorative bottles with tight-fitting lids. Store at room temperature for up to 1 month. To serve, pour over crushed ice in small glass. Makes about 4 1/3 cups (1.1 L).

*1 oz. **(30 mL):** 84 Calories; 0 g Total Fat (0 g Mono, 0 g Poly, 0 g Sat); 0 mg Cholesterol; 14 g Carbohydrate; trace Fibre; 0 g Protein; 1 mg Sodium*

cranberry liqueur

The bouquet will say "gin," but the taste will say "cranberry."

Fresh (or frozen, thawed) cranberries, coarsely chopped	4 cups	1 L
Granulated sugar	3 cups	750 mL
Gin	2 cups	500 mL
Vanilla extract	1 tsp.	5 mL

Combine all 4 ingredients in large sterile jar with tight-fitting lid. Let stand at room temperature for 6 weeks, shaking well once per week. Strain through sieve into 4 cup (1 L) liquid measure. Discard solids. Return liquid to same jar. Store in cool location for up to 2 months. Makes about 3 1/2 cups (875 L).

1/4 cup (60 mL): 259 Calories; 0.1 g Total Fat (0 g Mono, 0 g Poly, 0 g Sat); 0 mg Cholesterol; 48 g Carbohydrate; 1 g Fibre; trace Protein; 1 mg Sodium

ESPECIALLY
FOR
YOUR
BRIDAL
SHOWER

creamy cranberry punch

A blend of fruit and yogurt, this creamy drink is a healthy option for kids and adults.

Boxes of whole frozen strawberries (10 oz., 300 g, each), thawed	2	2
Cranberry cocktail, chilled	1 1/3 cups	325 mL
Plain yogurt	1 1/3 cups	325 mL
Small bananas, cut up	3	3
Granulated sugar	1/2 cup	125 mL
Cranberry cocktail, chilled	5 1/2 cups	1.4 L
Orange juice	1/3 cup	75 mL

Process first 5 ingredients in blender until smooth. Pour into punch bowl.

Add second amount of cranberry cocktail and orange juice. Stir. Makes about 10 cups (2.5 L).

1 cup (250 mL): 234 Calories; 1.5 g Total Fat (0.4 g Mono, 0.2 g Poly, 0.8 g Sat); 4 mg Cholesterol; 57 g Carbohydrate; 2 g Fibre; 2 g Protein; 20 mg Sodium

walnut cranberry salad
with sweet mustard dressing

A wonderful accompaniment to lean cuts of meat such as chicken breasts or pork tenderloin, this salad can also be made with baby spinach leaves instead of mixed greens. Make the dressing ahead of time so the flavours get to know each other.

DRESSING		
Olive (or cooking) oil	1/3 cup	75 mL
White wine vinegar	3 tbsp.	50 mL
Brown sugar, packed	1 tbsp.	15 mL
Chopped fresh oregano (or 3/4 tsp., 4 mL, dried)	1 tbsp.	15 mL
Prepared mustard	2 tsp.	10 mL
Garlic clove, minced (or 1/4 tsp., 1 mL, powder)	1	1
Salt	1/4 tsp.	1 mL
Pepper	1/4 tsp.	1 mL
SALAD		
Mixed salad greens	8 cups	2 L
Dried cranberries	1/2 cup	125 mL
Walnut halves, coarsely chopped	1/2 cup	125 mL
Goat (chèvre) cheese, chopped (see Tip, page 64)	4 1/2 oz.	125 g
Bacon slices, cooked crisp and crumbled	6	6

Dressing: Combine all 8 ingredients in small jar with tight-fitting lid. Shake well. Makes about 1/2 cup (125 mL) dressing.

Salad: Combine first 3 ingredients in large bowl. Sprinkle with cheese and bacon. Drizzle dressing over top. Toss. Makes about 10 cups (2.5 L).

1 cup (250 mL): 190 Calories; 15.8 g Total Fat (13.1 g Mono, 5.8 g Poly, 6.0 g Sat); 15.9 mg Cholesterol; 9 g Carbohydrate; 2 g Fibre; 6 g Protein; 189 mg Sodium

cranberry brie salad

Chewy, port-infused cranberries contrast wonderfully with soft bites of Brie and crunchy croutons.

Dried cranberries	1/2 cup	125 mL
Port wine	1/4 cup	60 mL
Head of butter lettuce, cut or torn	1	1
Croutons	2/3 cup	150 mL
Brie cheese, chopped	4 oz.	125 g
CRANBERRY DRESSING		
Cranberry cocktail	2 tbsp.	30 mL
Olive (or cooking) oil	2 tbsp.	30 mL
Basil pesto	1 tbsp.	15 mL
Red wine vinegar	1 tbsp.	15 mL

Measure cranberries and wine into small bowl. Stir until coated. Let stand for 1 hour, stirring occasionally. Drain. Transfer cranberries to large bowl.

Add next 3 ingredients. Toss.

Cranberry Dressing: Combine all 4 ingredients in jar with tight-fitting lid. Shake well. Makes about 1/3 cup (75 mL) dressing. Drizzle over salad. Toss gently. Serves 4.

1 serving: 245 Calories; 17.3 g Total Fat (8.8 g Mono, 1.1 g Poly, 6.4 g Sat); 28 mg Cholesterol; 14 g Carbohydrate; 3 g Fibre; 8 g Protein; 269 mg Sodium

hot turkey sandwich

Some people believe the leftovers are the best part of a turkey dinner! Toast the bread for a crispier sandwich.

Cold turkey gravy	2 tbsp.	30 mL
Whole-wheat bread slice	1	1
Prepared stuffing	3 tbsp.	50 mL
Sliced cooked turkey	2 oz.	57 g
Canned whole cranberry sauce, mashed	2 tbsp.	30 mL
Whole-wheat bread slice	1	1
Cold turkey gravy, thinned with a little hot water	1/4 cup	60 mL
Pepper, sprinkle		

Spread first amount of gravy over first bread slice. Place on microwave-safe plate.

Sprinkle stuffing over gravy. Arrange turkey over top. Spread cranberry sauce over turkey. Microwave, covered, on medium (50%) for 2 minutes.

Place second bread slice over cranberry sauce. Pour second amount of gravy over top. Microwave, uncovered, on medium (50%) for 1 minute. Sprinkle with pepper. Let stand for 1 minute. Makes 1 sandwich.

1 sandwich: 368 Calories; 9.2 g Total Fat (2.9 g Mono, 2.8 g Poly, 1.9 g Sat); 32 mg Cholesterol; 53 g Carbohydrate; 3 g Fibre; 17 g Protein; 1520 mg Sodium

continental chicken

No slow cooker? Just pop everything into an ungreased 4 quart (4 L) casserole and bake, covered, in a 325°F (160°C) oven for 1 1/2 to 2 hours until the chicken is tender. Brighten up your lunch by using the remaining cranberry sauce as a spread for cheese sandwiches.

Boneless, skinless chicken breast halves (4 – 6 oz., 113 – 170 g, each)	12	12
Canned whole cranberry sauce	1 1/4 cups	300 mL
French dressing	1/2 cup	125 mL
Envelope of onion soup mix (1 1/4 oz., 38 g), stir before dividing	1/2	1/2
Granulated sugar	1 tbsp.	15 mL
Pepper	1/8 tsp.	0.5 mL

Place chicken breast halves in 5 quart (5 L) slow cooker.

Combine remaining 5 ingredients in small bowl. Spoon over chicken. Cook, covered, on Low for 8 to 10 hours or on High for 4 to 5 hours. Serves 12.

1 serving: 224 Calories; 5.9 g Total Fat (4.2 g Mono, 2.7 g Poly, 1.1 g Sat); 108.5 mg Cholesterol; 15 g Carbohydrate; trace Fibre; 27 g Protein; 415 mg Sodium

duck with cranberry and sage

Allow yourself enough time to marinate the duck the night before. Creamy mashed potatoes and buttered snow peas or Brussels sprouts complement this dish nicely.

Whole duck, approximately	5 lbs.	2.3 kg
Cranberry cocktail	1 cup	250 mL
Canned whole cranberry sauce	1/2 cup	125 mL
Dry (or alcohol-free) white wine	1/2 cup	125 mL
Chopped fresh sage	3 tbsp.	50 mL
Salt	1/2 tsp.	2 mL
Pepper	1/2 tsp.	2 mL

Place duck, backbone-up, on cutting board. Cut down both sides of backbone, using kitchen shears or knife, to remove. Turn duck over. Press duck flat. Cut duck in half through breastbone. Cut each half into 2 pieces. Place in large shallow dish.

Combine remaining 6 ingredients in small bowl. Pour over duck. Stir or turn to coat. Let stand, covered, in refrigerator for at least 6 hours or overnight, turning occasionally. Drain, reserving cranberry mixture in medium saucepan. Place duck, skin-side up, on greased wire rack set in large roasting pan. Prick skin all over with metal skewer being careful not to pierce through to flesh. Bake, uncovered, in 300°F (150°C) oven for about 2 1/2 hours until duck is tender and skin is crisp. Bring marinade to a boil. Reduce heat to medium. Boil gently, uncovered, for about 20 minutes, stirring occasionally, until thickened. Makes about 3/4 cup (175 mL) sauce. Serve with duck. Serves 4.

1 serving (without skin): 360 Calories; 13.7 g Total Fat (4.5 g Mono, 1.7 g Poly, 5.1 g Sat); 108 mg Cholesterol; 25 g Carbohydrate; trace Fibre; 29 g Protein; 390 mg Sodium

stuffing balls

Colourful, chewy and sweet, these are a terrific change from regular stuffing.

Cooking oil	1 tbsp.	15 mL
Medium onion, chopped	1	1
Chopped celery	1/2 cup	125 mL
Coarse dry bread crumbs	6 cups	1.5 L
Dried cranberries	1 1/2 cups	375 mL
Parsley flakes	2 tsp.	10 mL
Poultry seasoning	2 tsp.	10 mL
Salt	1 tsp.	5 mL
Pepper	1/4 tsp.	1 mL
Large eggs, fork-beaten	3	3
Water	3/4 cup	175 mL
Hard margarine (or butter), melted	1/3 cup	75 mL

Heat cooking oil in medium frying pan on medium-high. Add onion and celery. Cook for 5 to 10 minutes, stirring often, until onion is softened. Transfer to large bowl.

Add next 6 ingredients. Stir well.

Add eggs and water. Stir. Mix well. Roll into 10 balls, using about 1/2 cup (125 mL) mixture for each. Arrange in single layer in small greased roasting pan.

Drizzle with margarine. Bake, covered, in 350°F (175°C) oven for about 25 minutes until golden. Makes 10 stuffing balls.

1 stuffing ball: 403 Calories; 13.2 g Total Fat (7.0 g Mono, 2.3 g Poly, 2.7 g Sat); 64.7 mg Cholesterol; 60 g Carbohydrate; 6 g Fibre; 11 g Protein; 928 mg Sodium

cran-orange chutney

A beautiful, ruby-red combination spiced to taste like Christmas, this preserve is an excellent alternative to plain cranberry sauce for the holiday turkey. Makes a thoughtful hostess gift.

Fresh (or frozen, thawed) cranberries	2 cups	500 mL
Cranberry cocktail	1/2 cup	125 mL
Medium peeled oranges, coarsely chopped	2	2
Golden raisins	1/3 cup	75 mL
Chopped onion	1/4 cup	60 mL
Brown sugar, packed	1 cup	250 mL
Apple cider vinegar	1/2 cup	125 mL
Ground cloves	1/2 tsp.	2 mL
Ground ginger	1/2 tsp.	2 mL
Salt	1/2 tsp.	2 mL
Pepper	1/2 tsp.	2 mL
Ground cinnamon	1/4 tsp.	1 mL

Combine first 5 ingredients in large saucepan. Bring to a boil. Reduce heat to medium-low. Simmer, uncovered, for about 2 minutes until cranberries are softened.

Add remaining 7 ingredients. Stir. Bring to a boil. Reduce heat to medium-low. Simmer, uncovered, for 50 to 60 minutes, stirring occasionally, until slightly thickened. Remove from heat. Gently mash cranberries. Fill 5 hot sterile 1/2 cup (125 mL) jars to within 1/2 inch (12 mm) of top. Wipe rims of jars. Place sterile metal lids on jars and screw on metal bands fingertip tight. Do not over-tighten. Process in boiling water bath for 15 minutes (see Note). Remove jars. Cool. Chill after opening. Makes about 2 1/2 cups (625 mL).

1 tbsp. (15 mL): 33 Calories; 0 g Total Fat (0 g Mono, 0 g Poly, 0 g Sat); 0 mg Cholesterol; 9 g Carbohydrate; trace Fibre; 0 g Protein; 31 mg Sodium

Note: Processing time is for elevations 1001 to 3000 feet (306 to 915 m) above sea level. Make adjustment for elevation in your area if necessary.

cranberry cornbread

So quick to make, this cornbread is best served warm, but it freezes well after it has cooled. Instead of cutting it into simple squares, you can slice the cornbread into eight rectangles and then cut each rectangle on the diagonal to form triangles.

All-purpose flour	1 cup	250 mL
Yellow cornmeal	1 cup	250 mL
Baking powder	1 tbsp.	15 mL
Salt	1/2 tsp.	2 mL
Large egg	1	1
Hard margarine (or butter), melted	6 tbsp.	100 mL
Brown sugar, packed	1/2 cup	125 mL
Buttermilk (or soured milk, see Tip, page 64)	1 cup	250 mL
Coarsely chopped fresh (or frozen) cranberries	1 cup	250 mL
Chopped walnuts	2/3 cup	150 mL

Measure first 4 ingredients into large bowl. Stir. Make a well in centre.

Beat next 3 ingredients in medium bowl until smooth. Add buttermilk and cranberries. Stir. Add to well. Stir until just moistened. Spread in greased 9 x 9 inch (22 x 22 cm) pan.

Sprinkle with walnuts. Bake in 400°F (205°C) oven for about 25 minutes until wooden pick inserted in centre comes out clean. Cuts into 16 pieces.

1 piece: 178 Calories; 8.1 g Total Fat (3.6 g Mono, 2.7 g Poly, 1.4 g Sat); 14 mg Cholesterol; 23 g Carbohydrate; 1 g Fibre; 3 g Protein; 159 mg Sodium

fruit bread

Delicious served fresh out of the oven, or try it toasted for a special breakfast.

Milk	1 cup	250 mL
Granulated sugar	1/4 cup	60 mL
Envelope of active dry yeast (or 2 1/4 tsp., 11 mL)	1/4 oz.	8 g
All-purpose flour	1 cup	250 mL
Large egg, fork-beaten	1	1
Grated orange zest	1 tsp.	5 mL
Butter (or hard margarine), melted	1/2 cup	125 mL
Chopped walnuts, toasted (see Tip, page 64)	1/3 cup	75 mL
Currants	1/3 cup	75 mL
Dried cranberries	1/3 cup	75 mL
Golden raisins	1/3 cup	75 mL
Ground cinnamon	1/2 tsp.	2 mL
Salt	1/2 tsp.	2 mL
Ground nutmeg	1/4 tsp.	1 mL
All-purpose flour, approximately	2 cups	500 mL
Egg yolk (large), fork-beaten	1	1
White sanding (decorating) sugar (see Tip, page 64)	1 tbsp.	15 mL

Combine milk and granulated sugar in small heavy saucepan. Heat and stir on medium until sugar is dissolved. Pour into extra-large bowl. Let stand for 5 minutes.

Sprinkle yeast over top. Let stand for 10 minutes. Stir until yeast is dissolved.

Add first amount of flour. Stir until smooth. Cover with greased waxed paper and tea towel. Let stand in oven with light on and door closed for about 30 minutes until mixture forms a foamy, domed surface.

Add egg and orange zest. Stir well.

Add next 8 ingredients. Mix well.

Add second amount of flour. Mix until soft dough forms. Turn out onto lightly floured surface. Knead for 5 to 10 minutes until smooth and elastic, adding more flour, if necessary, to prevent sticking. Place in separate greased extra-large bowl, turning once to grease top. Cover with greased waxed paper and tea towel. Let stand in oven with light on and door closed for about 1 hour until doubled in bulk. Punch down dough. Turn out onto lightly floured surface. Knead for about 1 minute until smooth. Shape into loaf. Place in greased 9 x 5 x 3 inch (22 x 12.5 x 7.5 cm) loaf pan. Cover with greased waxed paper and tea towel. Let stand in oven with light on and door closed for about 30 minutes until doubled in size.

Brush top of loaf with egg yolk. Sprinkle with sanding sugar. Bake in 375°F (190°C) oven for 10 minutes. Reduce heat to 350°F (175°C). Bake for about 30 minutes until golden and hollow sounding when tapped. Remove loaf from pan and place on wire rack to cool. Cuts into 16 slices.

1 slice: 217 Calories; 8.8 g Total Fat (2.4 g Mono, 1.5 g Poly, 4.2 g Sat); 44 mg Cholesterol; 31 g Carbohydrate; 2 g Fibre; 5 g Protein; 150 mg Sodium

cranberry orange muffins

If you can bear to give some of these away, let them cool completely before
wrapping—a good rule to follow with all freshly baked items.

All-purpose flour	2 cups	500 mL
Baking powder	2 tsp.	10 mL
Baking soda	1/2 tsp.	2 mL
Salt	1/2 tsp.	2 mL
Large egg	1	1
Granulated sugar	1/2 cup	125 mL
Cooking oil	1/4 cup	60 mL
Chopped cranberries	1 cup	250 mL
Juice of 1 large orange, plus frozen concentrated orange juice, to make	3/4 cup	175 mL
Grated zest of 1 large orange (see Tip, page 64)		

Measure first 4 ingredients into large bowl. Stir. Make a well in centre. Set aside.

Beat next 3 ingredients in medium bowl.

Add remaining 3 ingredients. Stir well. Add to well in flour mixture. Stir until just moistened. Fill 12 greased muffin cups almost full. Bake in 400°F (205°C) oven for 15 to 20 minutes until wooden pick inserted in centre of muffin comes out clean. Let stand in pan for 5 minutes. Remove muffins from pan and place on wire rack to cool. Makes 12 muffins.

1 muffin: *214 Calories; 5.3 g Total Fat (2.9 g Mono, 1.6 g Poly, 0.5 g Sat); 16 mg Cholesterol; 39 g Carbohydrate; 1 g Fibre; 3 g Protein; 200 mg Sodium*

cranberry cheese muffins

Grab one of these and a glass of milk on busy mornings and you're good to go.

All-purpose flour	3 cups	750 mL
Grated sharp Cheddar cheese	1 1/2 cups	375 mL
Dried cranberries	1 cup	250 mL
Brown sugar, packed	3/4 cup	175 mL
Baking powder	1 tbsp.	15 mL
Ground cinnamon	1 tsp.	5 mL
Salt	1 tsp.	5 mL
Dried thyme	1/2 tsp.	2 mL
Large eggs	2	2
Milk	1 cup	250 mL
Cooking oil	1/3 cup	75 mL

Measure first 8 ingredients into large bowl. Stir. Make a well in centre.

Beat remaining 3 ingredients in medium bowl. Add to well. Stir until just moistened. Fill 12 greased muffin cups 3/4 full. Bake in 375°F (190°C) oven for 20 to 25 minutes until wooden pick inserted in centre of muffin comes out clean. Let stand in pan for 5 minutes. Remove muffins from pan and place on wire rack to cool. Makes 12 muffins.

1 muffin: 331 Calories; 12.8 g Total Fat (5.6 g Mono, 2.3 g Poly, 4.1 g Sat); 52 mg Cholesterol; 45 g Carbohydrate; 2 g Fibre; 9 g Protein; 411 mg Sodium

cranberry citrus loaf

Studded with nuts, colourful fruit and peel, this small loaf is irresistible when it comes out of the oven, but like many quick breads, it cuts better on the second day.

All-purpose flour	2 cups	500 mL
Baking powder	2 tsp.	10 mL
Salt	1/2 tsp.	2 mL
Hard margarine (or butter), softened	1/4 cup	60 mL
Granulated sugar	2/3 cup	150 mL
Large egg	1	1
Vanilla extract	1/2 tsp.	2 mL
Milk	3/4 cup	175 mL
Chopped pecans (or walnuts)	1/2 cup	125 mL
Chopped fresh (or frozen) cranberries	1/3 cup	75 mL
Chopped mixed glazed fruit	1/3 cup	75 mL
Golden raisins, coarsely chopped	1/3 cup	75 mL

Measure first 3 ingredients into large bowl. Stir. Make a well in centre. Set aside.

Cream margarine and sugar in separate large bowl. Add egg and vanilla. Beat well.

Add remaining 5 ingredients. Stir well. Add to well in flour mixture. Stir until just moistened. Spread in greased 8 x 4 x 3 inch (20 x 10 x 7.5 cm) loaf pan. Bake in 350°F (175°C) oven for about 1 hour until wooden pick inserted in centre comes out clean. Let stand in pan for 10 minutes. Remove loaf from pan and place on wire rack to cool. Cuts into 14 slices.

1 slice: 206 Calories; 7.2 g Total Fat (4.3 g Mono, 1.2 g Poly, 1.2 g Sat); 15.6 mg Cholesterol; 33 g Carbohydrate; 1 g Fibre; 3 g Protein; 191 mg Sodium

pumpkin cranberry loaf

Lining the pan with parchment paper allows you to remove the loaf from the pan without disturbing the syrup and pecan topping.

Dried cranberries	2/3 cup	150 mL
Orange juice	2/3 cup	150 mL
All-purpose flour	2 1/2 cups	625 mL
Baking powder	2 1/2 tsp.	12 mL
Baking soda	1 tsp.	5 mL
Salt	1/4 tsp.	1 mL
Butter (or hard margarine), softened	1/3 cup	75 mL
Brown sugar, packed	1/3 cup	75 mL
Large eggs	2	2
Can of pure pumpkin (no spices)	14 oz.	398 mL
Maple (or maple-flavoured) syrup	1 cup	250 mL
Maple (or maple-flavoured) syrup	1/2 cup	125 mL
Chopped pecans, toasted (see Tip, page 64)	3 tbsp.	50 mL

Combine cranberries and orange juice in small saucepan on medium. Heat and stir until just boiling. Remove from heat. Let stand for about 30 minutes until cooled to room temperature.

Measure next 4 ingredients into large bowl. Stir. Make a well in centre. Set aside.

Cream butter and brown sugar in medium bowl. Add eggs, 1 at a time, beating well after each addition.

Add pumpkin and first amount of syrup. Beat until smooth. Add to well in flour mixture. Add cranberry mixture. Stir until just moistened. Line bottom and sides of lightly greased 9 x 5 x 3 inch (22 x 12.5 x 7.5 cm) loaf pan with parchment (not waxed) paper, leaving 1 1/2 inch (3.8 cm) overhang on each side. Spread batter in pan. Bake in 350°F (175°C) oven for about 75 minutes until wooden pick inserted in centre comes out clean. Remove pan to wire rack. Run knife around loaf to loosen. Do not remove from pan.

Pour second amount of syrup into small heavy saucepan. Bring to a boil on medium. Boil gently, uncovered, for 3 to 5 minutes, stirring occasionally, until slightly reduced and thickened. Carefully pour hot syrup evenly over loaf.

Sprinkle with pecans. Let stand in pan on wire rack for 30 minutes. Lift loaf from pan using parchment paper edges as handles. Place loaf on wire rack to cool completely. Discard parchment paper. Cuts into 16 slices.

1 slice: 253 Calories; 6 g Total Fat (2 g Mono, 0.6 g Poly, 2.9 g Sat); 38 mg Cholesterol; 48 g Carbohydrate; 2 g Fibre; 4 g Protein; 231 mg Sodium

apple cranberry tart

If you don't want to cut out the pastry shapes by hand, you can use small cookie cutters to make a decorative top.

Pastry for 2 crust 9 inch (22 cm) pie

Thinly sliced peeled tart apple (such as Granny Smith)	7 cups	1.75 L
Water	1/4 cup	60 mL
Granulated sugar	2/3 cup	150 mL
Dried cranberries	1/3 cup	75 mL
Grated lemon zest	1 tsp.	5 mL
Egg white (large), fork-beaten	1	1
White sanding (decorating) sugar (optional), see Tip, page 64	2 tbsp.	30 mL

Roll out 3/4 of pastry on lightly floured surface to fit ungreased 9 inch (22 cm) tart pan with fluted side and removable bottom. Carefully lift pastry and press into bottom and up side pan. Trim edge. Place tart pan on ungreased baking sheet (see Tip, page 64). Chill, covered, for 1 hour.

Combine apple and water in large saucepan. Bring to a boil. Reduce heat to medium. Boil gently, covered, for about 8 minutes, stirring occasionally, until apple is tender.

Add next 3 ingredients. Stir. Remove from heat. Cool. Drain. Pour apple mixture into shell. Spread evenly. Roll out remaining pastry on lightly floured surface to about 1/8 inch (3 mm) thickness. Cut out pastry shapes. Place around edge of tart.

Brush pastry with egg white. Sprinkle with sanding sugar. Bake on bottom rack in 375ºF (190ºC) oven for about 45 minutes until golden. Cuts into 8 wedges.

1 wedge: 297 Calories; 10.7 g Total Fat (5 g Mono, 1.4 g Poly, 3.4 g Sat); 0 mg Cholesterol; 50 g Carbohydrate; 3 g Fibre; 2 g Protein; 212 mg Sodium

cran-raisin pie

Real whipping cream is a must to mellow the tangy/sweet flavour of this delicious pie.

Granulated sugar	2 1/4 cups	550 mL
All-purpose flour	1/3 cup	75 mL
Salt	3/4 tsp.	4 mL
Boiling water	1 1/2 cups	375 mL
Fresh (or frozen, thawed) cranberries	4 1/2 cups	1.1 L
Raisins	3 cups	750 mL
Vanilla extract	1 1/2 tsp.	7 mL
Unbaked 9 inch (22 cm) pie shells	2	2
Whipping cream	2 cups	500 mL
Granulated sugar	4 tsp.	20 mL
Vanilla extract	1 tsp.	5 mL

Combine first 3 ingredients in large heatproof bowl. Stir in boiling water.

Put cranberries and raisins into food processor. Pulse with on/off motion until finely chopped. Do not purée. Add to sugar mixture. Add first amount of vanilla. Stir.

Spread cranberry mixture evenly in pie shells. Bake on bottom rack in 350°F (175°C) oven for about 1 hour until crust is golden and filling is set. Cool.

Beat remaining 3 ingredients in small bowl until soft peaks form. Spread over pies. Each pie cuts into 8 wedges, for a total of 16 wedges.

1 wedge: 453 Calories; 18.6 g Total Fat (3.0 g Mono, 0.4 g Poly, 8.5 g Sat); 38 mg Cholesterol; 71 g Carbohydrate;2 g Fibre; 3 g Protein; 250 mg Sodium

cranberry cheesecake

Because this can chill overnight after baking, this delicious dessert frees up valuable time for you on the day of your party.

CRANBERRY TOPPING

Fresh (or frozen, thawed) cranberries	2 cups	500 mL
Cranberry cocktail	1 cup	250 mL
Grated orange zest	1/2 tsp.	2 mL
Granulated sugar	1/2 cup	125 mL
Cornstarch	1 1/2 tbsp.	25 mL
Ground cinnamon (optional)	1/8 tsp.	0.5 mL
Unflavoured gelatin	2 tsp.	10 mL
Orange liqueur	1 tbsp.	15 mL

CRUST

Hard margarine (or butter)	1/3 cup	75 mL
Ground cinnamon	1/4 tsp.	1 mL
Graham cracker crumbs	1 1/2 cups	375 mL

FILLING

Can of sweetened condensed milk	11 oz.	300 mL
Blocks of light cream cheese (8 oz., 250 g, each), softened	2	2
Grated orange zest	1 tsp.	5 mL
Vanilla extract	1 tsp.	5 mL
Dry curd cottage cheese	1 1/2 cups	375 mL
Orange juice	2 tbsp.	30 mL
Large eggs	4	4

Cranberry Topping: Combine first 3 ingredients in medium saucepan. Cook, covered, on medium-high for about 2 minutes until cranberries are softened. Reduce heat to medium-low.

Combine next 3 ingredients in small bowl. Add to cranberry mixture. Heat and stir until clear and slightly thickened.

Sprinkle gelatin over liqueur in separate small heatproof bowl. Let stand for 1 minute. Add to hot cranberry mixture. Stir until gelatin is dissolved. Chill. Makes about 2 cups (500 mL) topping.

Crust: Melt margarine in small saucepan on medium. Stir in cinnamon and graham crumbs. Mix well. Press into bottom and slightly up side of greased 10 inch (25 cm) springform pan.

Filling: Beat first 4 ingredients in large bowl until smooth.

Put cottage cheese, orange juice and 3/4 cup (175 mL) topping into food processor. Pulse with on/off motion until smooth. Add to cream cheese mixture. Beat well.

Add eggs, 1 at a time, beating well after each addition. Spread evenly over crust. Bake in 400°F (205°C) oven for 10 minutes. Reduce heat to 325°F (160°C). Bake for about 40 minutes until centre is almost set. Turn heat off. Let stand in oven for 10 minutes. Remove to wire rack. Run knife around inside edge of pan to allow cheesecake to settle evenly. Let stand in pan on wire rack until cooled completely. Chill for at least 6 hours or overnight. Spoon remaining topping onto individual servings. Cuts into 12 pieces.

1 piece: 401 Calories; 19.2 g Total Fat (7.9 g Mono, 1.3 g Poly, 8.4 g Sat); 110.3 mg Cholesterol; 44 g Carbohydrate; 1 g Fibre; 13 g Protein; 486 mg Sodium

cranberry orange bars

Tucked into a lunch bag, these crunchy bars with their tart orange filling make a satisfying break in the middle of the day.

Cold butter (or hard margarine), cut up	1 1/2 cups	375 mL
All-purpose flour	2 cups	500 mL
Quick-cooking rolled oats (not instant)	1 1/2 cups	375 mL
Brown sugar, packed	1 cup	250 mL
Medium unsweetened coconut	1 cup	250 mL
Grated orange zest	2 tsp.	10 mL
Baking soda	1 tsp.	5 mL
Ground ginger	1 tsp.	5 mL
Chopped pecans, toasted (see Tip, page 64)	1 cup	250 mL
FILLING		
Can of whole cranberry sauce	14 oz.	398 mL
Orange marmalade	1 cup	250 mL

Cut butter into flour in large bowl until mixture resembles coarse crumbs.

Add next 6 ingredients. Stir well. Press half of oat mixture evenly in greased 10 x 15 inch (25 x 38 cm) jelly roll pan. Set aside.

Add pecans to remaining oat mixture. Stir. Set aside.

Filling: Combine cranberry sauce and marmalade in medium bowl. Spread evenly over oat mixture in pan. Sprinkle with reserved pecan mixture. Press down lightly. Bake in 350°F (175°C) oven for about 30 minutes until golden. Let stand in pan on wire rack to cool. Cut into 1 x 1 1/2 inch (2.5 x 3.8 cm) pieces. Makes 90 bars.

1 bar: 88 Calories; 4.9 g Total Fat (1.5 g Mono, 0.4 g Poly, 2.7 g Sat); 9 mg Cholesterol; 11 g Carbohydrate; trace Fibre; 1 g Protein; 52 mg Sodium

cranberry almond biscotti

Linger over that second cup of coffee with a few of these miniature goodies,
or bring your co-workers a jarful to celebrate a special event.

All-purpose flour	1 3/4 cups	425 mL
Granulated sugar	2/3 cup	150 mL
Baking powder	1/2 tsp.	2 mL
Salt	1/4 tsp.	1 mL
Cold hard margarine (or butter), cut up	1/3 cup	75 mL
Large eggs	2	2
Almond extract	1/2 tsp.	2 mL
Dried cranberries	2/3 cup	150 mL
Whole natural almonds	2/3 cup	150 mL

Combine first 4 ingredients in large bowl. Cut in margarine until mixture resembles coarse crumbs. Make a well in centre.

Beat eggs and extract with fork in small bowl until frothy. Add to well. Mix until stiff dough forms. Turn out onto lightly floured surface. Shape dough into ball. Flatten slightly.

Sprinkle cranberries and almonds over top. Press down lightly. Fold dough in half to enclose cranberries and almonds. Knead for 1 to 2 minutes until evenly distributed. Divide dough into 4 equal portions. Shape each portion into 6 inch (15 cm) long log. Place logs crosswise on greased cookie sheet about 2 inches (5 cm) apart. Flatten logs slightly. Bake in 350°F (175°C) oven for about 20 minutes until golden. Let stand on cookie sheet for about 20 minutes until cool enough to handle. Using serrated knife, cut logs diagonally into 1/2 inch (12 mm) slices. Arrange evenly spaced apart on greased cookie sheets. Reduce heat to 300°F (150°C). Bake for about 20 minutes, turning at halftime, until dry and crisp. Let stand on cookie sheets for 5 minutes. Remove biscotti from cookie sheets and place on wire racks to cool. Makes about 42 biscotti.

1 biscotti: 66 Calories; 3 g Total Fat (1.8 g Mono, 0.5 g Poly, 0.5 g Sat); 10 mg Cholesterol;
9 g Carbohydrate; 1 g Fibre; 1 g Protein; 40 mg Sodium

cranberry macadamia mounds

When only the best will do, these are sure to impress!

Dried cranberries	1 1/2 cups	375 mL
Orange juice	1/2 cup	125 mL
Orange liqueur	2 tbsp.	30 mL
All-purpose flour	3 cups	750 mL
Brown sugar, packed	1 1/2 cups	375 mL
Coarsely chopped macadamia nuts, toasted (see Tip, page 64)	1 cup	250 mL
White chocolate chips	1 cup	250 mL
Baking powder	1 1/2 tbsp.	25 mL
Salt	1/2 tsp.	2 mL
Large egg	1	1
Buttermilk (or soured milk, see Tip, page 64)	1 cup	250 mL
Hard margarine (or butter), melted	2/3 cup	150 mL
Grated orange zest (see Tip, page 64)	1 tbsp.	15 mL

Combine first 3 ingredients in small bowl. Let stand for 30 minutes, stirring occasionally. Drain.

Measure next 6 ingredients into large bowl. Stir. Make a well in centre.

Beat remaining 4 ingredients with whisk in separate small bowl. Add to well. Add cranberries. Stir until just moistened. Drop, using 1 1/2 tbsp. (25 mL) for each, about 2 inches (5 cm) apart onto greased cookie sheets. Bake in 375°F (190°C) oven for 10 to 12 minutes until just golden and wooden pick inserted in centre comes out clean. Let stand on cookie sheets for 5 minutes. Remove cookies from cookie sheets and place on wire racks to cool. Makes about 72 cookies.

1 cookie: 90 Calories; 4.2 g Total Fat (2.6 g Mono, 0.3 g Poly, 1.1 g Sat); 4 mg Cholesterol; 12 g Carbohydrate; 1 g Fibre; 1 g Protein; 70 mg Sodium

cranberry white chocolate cookies

Delightfully decadent! Cranberries and white chocolate are a perfect pair.

Large eggs	2	2
Brown sugar, packed	1 3/4 cups	425 mL
Cooking oil	1/2 cup	125 mL
Vanilla extract	1 tsp.	5 mL
All-purpose flour	1 3/4 cups	425 mL
Baking powder	1 tsp.	5 mL
Baking soda	1/2 tsp.	2 mL
Dried cranberries	1 cup	250 mL
White chocolate chips	1 cup	250 mL

Beat eggs and brown sugar in large bowl until thick and pale. Add cooking oil and vanilla. Beat until smooth.

Combine next 3 ingredients in small bowl. Add to brown sugar mixture in 2 additions, mixing well after each addition until no dry flour remains.

Add cranberries and chocolate chips. Mix well. Chill, covered, for 1 hour. Roll into balls, using 1 tbsp. (15 mL) for each. Arrange about 2 inches (5 cm) apart on greased cookie sheets. Bake in 375ºF (190ºC) oven for about 10 minutes until golden. Let stand on cookie sheets for 5 minutes. Remove cookies from cookie sheets and place on wire racks to cool. Makes about 48 cookies.

1 cookie: 98 Calories; 3.8 g Total Fat (1.9 g Mono, 0.8 g Poly, 0.9 g Sat); 10 mg Cholesterol; 15 g Carbohydrate; 1 g Fibre; 1 g Protein; 31 mg Sodium

new year's fritters

Many different cultures have a similar recipe—oliebollen in Holland and Portzelky within the Mennonite community are versions of this yummy snack.

Dried cranberries	1/2 cup	125 mL
Diced dried apricot	1/2 cup	125 mL
Golden raisins	1/2 cup	125 mL
Boiling water	2 cups	500 mL
Chopped glazed red and/or green cherries	1/2 cup	125 mL
Large eggs, room temperature	3	3
Granulated sugar	3 tbsp.	50 mL
Salt	1/2 tsp.	2 mL
Hot milk	1 1/2 cups	375 mL
Hard margarine (or butter)	1 tbsp.	15 mL
All-purpose flour	2 cups	500 mL
Instant yeast	1 tbsp.	15 mL
All-purpose flour, approximately	2 cups	500 mL
Cooking oil, for deep-frying		
Icing (confectioner's) sugar (optional)		

Combine first 3 ingredients in small heatproof bowl. Add boiling water. Let stand for 5 minutes. Drain well. Spread fruit on dry tea towel or paper towels. Let stand until no moisture remains. Return to same bowl.

Add cherries. Stir.

Beat next 3 ingredients with fork in large bowl. Slowly stir in milk. Add margarine. Stir until margarine is melted. Mixture should feel very warm but not hot.

Combine first amount of flour and yeast in separate small bowl. Stir into egg mixture. Stir vigorously for 2 to 3 minutes until batter is smooth, very sticky and yeast is dissolved. Stir in fruit mixture.

Add second amount of flour, 1/2 cup (125 mL) at a time, mixing well after each addition until dough pulls away from side of bowl. Place dough in separate greased large bowl, turning once to grease top. Cover with greased waxed paper and tea towel. Let stand in oven with light on and door closed for about 1 hour until doubled in bulk. Punch dough down.

Deep-fry 4 to 5 rounded tablespoonfuls in hot (375°F, 190°C) cooking oil for 4 to 4 1/2 minutes, turning to cook evenly, until deep golden. Remove fritters to paper towels to drain. Repeat with remaining dough.

Sprinkle with icing sugar. Makes about 60 fritters.

1 fritter: 77 Calories; 2.9 g Total Fat (1.6 g Mono, 0.8 g Poly, 0.3 g Sat); 11 mg Cholesterol; 11 g Carbohydrate; 1 g Fibre; 2 g Protein; 29 mg Sodium

cranberry almond bark

Homemade chocolate bark may not be much less expensive than store-bought, but it tastes so much better!

White chocolate bars (3 1/2 oz., 100 g, each), chopped	5	5
Whole natural almonds	1 1/2 cups	375 mL
Dried cranberries	1 cup	250 mL

Heat chocolate in medium heavy saucepan on lowest heat, stirring often, until chocolate is almost melted. Do not overheat. Remove from heat. Stir until smooth.

Add almonds and cranberries. Stir until coated. Spread on waxed paper-lined baking sheet with sides to 1/4 inch (6 mm) thickness. Chill until set. Break into irregular-shaped pieces, about 1 1/2 x 2 inches (3.8 x 5 cm) each. Makes about 56 pieces.

1 piece: 75 Calories; 4.8 g Total Fat (2.2 g Mono, 0.5 g Poly, 1.8 g Sat); 2 mg Cholesterol; 7 g Carbohydrate; 1 g Fibre; 1 g Protein; 8 mg Sodium

chocolate cranberry rum balls

These white chocolate rum balls with a cranberry twist make an interesting visual contrast to dark or milk chocolate confections.

Dried cranberries	1 cup	250 mL
Dark (navy) rum	1/3 cup	75 mL
Finely crushed vanilla wafers (about 70 wafers)	2 1/2 cups	625 mL
Ground pecans, toasted (see Tip, page 64)	1 1/2 cups	375 mL
Hard margarine (or butter), melted	1/3 cup	75 mL
Icing (confectioner's) sugar	1/3 cup	75 mL
White chocolate baking squares (1 oz., 28 g, each), chopped	14	14
Chocolate sprinkles (optional)		

Combine cranberries and rum in small bowl. Let stand for 1 hour.

Combine next 4 ingredients in large bowl. Add cranberry mixture. Mix well. Roll into balls, using 1 tbsp. (15 mL) for each. Place on waxed paper-lined baking sheet with sides. Chill for about 1 hour until firm.

Heat chocolate in small heavy saucepan on lowest heat, stirring often, until almost melted. Do not overheat. Remove from heat. Stir until smooth. Place 1 ball on top of fork. Dip into chocolate until coated, allowing excess to drip back into pan. Place on same baking sheet. Repeat with remaining balls and chocolate.

Sprinkle chocolate sprinkles over balls before white chocolate sets. Chill for 1 hour. Makes about 50 balls.

1 ball: 108 Calories; 6.8 g Total Fat (3.4 g Mono, 1 g Poly, 2 g Sat); 4 mg Cholesterol; 10 g Carbohydrate; 1 g Fibre; 1 g Protein; 35 mg Sodium

recipe index

topical tips

Cutting or grating soft cheese: To grate or chop soft cheese easily, place in the freezer for 15 to 20 minutes until very firm.

Making soured milk: To make soured milk, measure 1 tbsp. (15 mL) white vinegar or lemon juice into a 1 cup (250 mL) liquid measure. Add enough milk to make 1 cup (250 mL). Stir. Let stand for 1 minute.

Sanding (decorating) sugar: Sanding sugar is a coarse decorating sugar that comes in white and various colours and is available at specialty kitchen stores.

Tart pan safety: Placing the tart pan on a baking sheet provides a safe way to remove the hot pan from the oven.

Toasting nuts, seeds or coconut: Cooking times will vary for each type of nut—so never toast them together. For small amounts, place ingredient in an ungreased shallow frying pan. Heat on medium for 3 to 5 minutes, stirring often, until golden. For larger amounts, spread ingredient evenly in an ungreased shallow pan. Bake in 350ºF (175ºC) oven for 5 to 10 minutes, stirring or shaking often, until golden.

Zest first; juice second: When a recipe calls for grated zest and juice, it's easier to grate the fruit first, then juice it. Be careful not to grate down to the pith (white part of the peel), which is bitter and best avoided.

Nutrition Information Guidelines

Each recipe is analyzed using the Canadian Nutrient File from Health Canada, which is based on the United States Department of Agriculture (USDA) Nutrient Database.

- If more than one ingredient is listed (such as "butter or hard margarine"), or if a range is given (1 – 2 tsp., 5 – 10 mL), only the first ingredient or first amount is analyzed.

- For meat, poultry and fish, the serving size per person is based on the recommended 4 oz. (113 g) uncooked weight (without bone), which is 2 – 3 oz. (57 – 85 g) cooked weight (without bone)— approximately the size of a deck of playing cards.

- Milk used is 1% M.F. (milk fat), unless otherwise stated.

- Cooking oil used is canola oil, unless otherwise stated.

- Ingredients indicating "sprinkle," "optional," or "for garnish" are not included in the nutrition information.

- The fat in recipes and combination foods can vary greatly depending on the sources and types of fats used in each specific ingredient. For these reasons, the count of saturated, monounsaturated and polyunsaturated fats may not add up to the total fat content.